THE ~~ROADS~~ ROAD

to

HOME OWNERSHIP

&

FINANCIAL FREEDOM

*How Choosing the Right Home
Loan and Avoiding Mortgage
Mistakes Can Save You Thousands*

JoAnn Cooper

Copyright ©2018 JoAnn Cooper

No part of this publication may be reproduced, stored in a retrieval system or transmitted in any way by any means, electronic, mechanical, photocopy, recording or otherwise without the prior permission of the author except as provided by USA copyright law.

This book is designed to provide accurate and authoritative information with regard to the subject matter covered. This information is given with the understanding that the author is not engaged in rendering legal or professional advice. Since the details of your situation are fact dependent, you should additionally seek the services of a competent professional.

ISBN-13:978-1720363385
ISBN-10: 1720363382

Published by E&D Publishing

Printed in the United States of America

Table of contents

Section:	Pages
Section 1... 1	
What to Do and Where to Start? 1	
Section 2: 5	
How to Prepare 5	
Credit Score 9	
Debt-to-Income Ratio (DTI) 11	
Low on Funds? 15	
Gifts, Down Payment Assistance, 401k Loans 16	
Low on Monthly Cash Flow? 20	
Never Paid for Living Expenses Before? 21	
Section 3: 23	
Choosing the Right Loan and Lender 23	
USDA (United States Department Of Agriculture) 25	
VA/VALB (Veterans Administration / Veterans Administration Land Board) 26	
FHA (Federal Housing Administration) 28	
Conventional & Jumbo 31	
Programs for Teachers, Firefighters, Police, or any other group. . 33	
How Many Things Can Go Wrong? Let Me Count the Ways…... 35	
Underwriters and Letters of Explanation.......................... 36	
Section 4: 39	
Buying or Building 39	
First Home You Will Ever Buy? 39	
Building a Home is Not for Everyone 41	

Section 5: 45
Positioning Yourself for Financial Freedom & Saving Thousands
.... 45
Last Home You Will Ever Buy? 45
Already Have Paid Off a Home? 47
Selling a Home? Don't Get Too Excited! 48
Can't See the Forest for the Trees? 50
The Real Value to Your Home Equity 52
When You Inherit a Home, the Gift May Be More Than "Just" a
Free Home 54

Section 6 57
Buyer Beware 57
Taxes, Insurance, & Homeowners' Associations – I thought I had a
Fixed Rate Loan! 57
Beware of Agreements to be Signed Outside of Closing 61

Dedication

This book is dedicated to my husband, Danny, and son, Ricky, in honor of all the love and support they have shown me over the years. Leaving a full-time, good-paying job, to start a new, commission-only career is a scary endeavor. It takes a lot of hard work and determination, but it also takes a strong support system. My family was, and continues to be, that support system. They endured me working long hours, on holidays, weekends, and vacations. They saw me through all the stresses that come with this job and I wouldn't have made it without them!

Thank you and Love you always!

JoAnn (Mom)

Section 1

What to Do and Where to Start?

So, you want to buy a home.

That's great! But... where do you start?

Do you scour the home listings in your city to find the perfect home?

Do you hire a real estate professional and start driving neighborhoods?

All in due time, my friend. The very first thing you should do is make sure you can BUY that perfect home- BEFORE you find it. There would be nothing worse than spending all your weekends looking at homes,

THE ~~ROADS~~ ROAD to HOME OWNERSHIP & FINANCIAL FREEDOM

falling in love with THE one, and then applying for your loan, only to find out you don't qualify. For instance, it will be a heartbreaking experience if you ever fall in love with a $300,000 home, only to find out you only qualify for a $200,000 home. Do you think any $200,000 home is going to satisfy you, after you have been shopping in a much higher price range? The order of things is very important. Timing is also very important.

Getting pre-qualified for your loan prior to shopping is great, but when? If there is incorrect information on your credit report, that could take months to correct. If you are receiving gift funds towards your down payment, it may take some time to properly document them in such a way to minimize paperwork and protect your donor's privacy.

As soon as you have even the slightest thought that you will be a homebuyer in the coming year, talk to a loan officer. You will be advised of what to do, and more importantly, what not to do, between now and the big day. Many people wait until they are ready to go under contract, or even ARE under contract, to apply. That makes the whole process more stressful for everyone involved, and in many cases, things come up that needed to be addressed weeks or months before.

Some issues can be overcome but will require lots more paperwork. Some things cannot be fixed at that late date and can end the dream with a startling reality check.

And, please don't make the mistake of thinking that this would only happen to people with little funds, or low credit scores. Yes, those folks have their challenges; but sometimes, the most successful folks have these issues, simply because of their success. In other words, the more companies you own, the more funds you are moving around in your accounts, the more business write-offs you have, the more likely you are to not have a straightforward loan application. These will be things we need to address and the earlier the better!

"Home Ownership is possible for just about everyone. You just need to have the right team in place and your home ownership dream will become a reality."

-JoAnn Cooper

Section 2:

How to Prepare

As you can imagine, the mortgage approval is based on a combination of factors. Everything from your employment history, credit score, income, and debt, to whether you will buy a single-family home, condo, townhouse, or mobile home will be taken into account.

How do you make sure your scenario looks as good as possible?

1. Keep records — everything in your loan file must be documented. Make sure you have paystubs, tax returns, W2s, and bank statements on hand, as well as documentation for any special circumstances you may have. If you don't do this, and you can't document a certain aspect of your financial picture, it can be fatal. For instance, if you deposit a large sum of money into your bank account and can't document with a paper trail, the Underwriter (UW) will not allow that money to be used for closing, which can cause you to be short on funds to close.

2. Consistency — longevity is important when it

comes to employment, residency, and credit. Don't close old credit cards or bank accounts, and don't change jobs, unless absolutely necessary prior to closing. For instance, if you change jobs in the middle of a transaction, the UW may want to see that you have been on the new job for a month before you can close. You may even have to provide a paystub, showing 30 days of income, which can take 6-8 weeks to receive on a new job. That can cause a severe delay and you can possibly lose the home to another buyer.

3. Responsibility — How you handle things in your life indicates how you will handle your mortgage. Bad things happen to the best of us. If there are negatives in your past, that is not necessarily a deal breaker. A legitimate explanation of the circumstance and your steps taken to ensure it doesn't happen again may go a long way. For instance, if you had to leave town for work and you left a family member in charge of your bills, and they didn't do a great job handling that responsibility for you, you may have late payments on your credit report. The UW doesn't want to hear that it's all his fault and you had no part in the problem. Instead, you need to submit a letter that explains what happened, says you made a bad decision to expect anyone else to care about your finances as much as you

do, and what you have since done to ensure it never happens again (e.g. set up automatic bill pay, or online banking bill pay, or auto drafts). Get the idea? Document that this is what happened, and this is what I did to fix the problem.

4. Knowledge — Different properties carry different costs and qualifications for loan approval. If you are changing your mind on the type of property you want to buy, keep your lender in the loop. Changes to property type, price range, or different property tax rates can significantly change how much home you qualify for. If you are prequalified for a single-family home, with an annual Homeowner's Association fee of $600, and then decide to buy a mobile home on acreage with no HOA, that doesn't mean an easier approval. Some loan programs don't allow for mobile homes and those that do, may have stricter requirements and very different rates. Also, if you decide to go from a single-family home with a $600/year HOA fee to a condo with a $400/month HOA fee, your payment will be significantly impacted and your prequalification may be invalid.

5. Involvement of Professionals — You cannot possibly know all there is to know about the loan process. It is so important for you to have a professional in your corner, to help you navigate through the process, and answer all your questions.

Also, a good mortgage professional will give you choices, and not just TELL you what your rate/terms/fees are. There is always more than one option and with a payment that will last you the next 30 years, you should be in on the decision-making process. Choose the lender who responds to your needs in a timely manner and with patience. The last thing you want to do is just blindly go along with the process and then, a year or two down the road, realize that you would have been better off doing something totally different. For instance, some lenders will see what funds you have on deposit and decide for you that a 20% down payment is the way to go to avoid mortgage insurance (MI). But, what if you have a child about to go to college next year, and a 3.5% or 5% down payment loan would leave you a lump sum of money to make the college years much more comfortable? Remember, just like there is not one interest rate for everyone, there is not just one loan option either. You should feel comfortable talking to your lender about what is important to you and what you want. If it's not possible, they will let you know, but you have a right to lay it out and have someone on your side, willing to try to make it work for you.

Credit Score

Your credit score is important because it is a combination of:
- How much credit you have to use
- How much you actually use
- How you pay back your obligations and
- How long you have had your credit history

It is a strong indication of how you will handle your affairs in the future.

Take great care of your credit score, as it affects almost everything in your life! From the obvious — interest rates and/or credit approvals — to everything else, from what you pay for insurance, to whether or not you get that job you want, and everything in between. Do you have kids going to college? Will you need to cosign for their apartment? If your credit isn't in good shape, they may be living in the dorm all 4 years, which is usually more expensive than apartment living.

Your credit says a lot about you. Protect it. If it's in poor health, repair it. If you don't know, find out. Ignorance is not bliss in the credit world. It affects too much for it to be ignored.

Don't max out your credit cards. Using all available credit gives the indication that you cannot make it on your income alone.

Pay everything on time, always. Even one late payment can decrease your scores significantly.

Check your report regularly for inaccurate information. Items that are reported incorrectly or attached to the wrong person's report can cause you problems that can take years to correct. Watch it carefully and report any problems immediately.

Folks who don't keep a close eye on their credit situation can be in for a terrible surprise when they apply for a mortgage. And, when that happens, fixing it generally takes much more than the 30 days they have until they are supposed to close on their new home!

That can be a devastating heartbreak.

Case in point:
I had a client who came to me early, which was very smart. Her credit score was not ideal. When we reviewed her credit report, we saw that she had several credit cards. Some were up to the limit and some had a very small percentage of the available limit used. I told her to transfer some of her higher balance cards to her lower balance cards and to try to make it to where all the balances were less than 30% of the limits (10% is ideal, but under 30% certainly is better than being maxed out). Once she did that, her score shot up 50 points, which allowed her to get into her home for a much lower interest rate and less scrutiny by the underwriter.

Debt-to-Income Ratio (DTI)

Your debt-to-income ratio is a large factor in mortgage approvals. That term simply refers to the amount of monthly debt payments you are obligated to pay to your creditors, divided by your gross monthly income, thus giving you a percentage. This percentage is your debt-to-income ratio or DTI.

So, if your car payment, credit card payments, student loan payments, and new mortgage (including principal, interest, taxes, insurance, MI, and HOA dues) add up to

THE ~~ROADS~~ ROAD to HOME OWNERSHIP & FINANCIAL FREEDOM

$3000/month and your gross income (before taxes or insurance deductions) is $7000/month, you would calculate your debt-to-income ratio this way...

$$3000 \text{ divided by } 7000 = .429 \text{ DTI}$$

This means that almost 43% of your GROSS income is dedicated to payments you are obligated to make each month. We all know another large portion of our income (usually 20-30%) goes to taxes, as well as deductions we have elected to have withheld from our paychecks for insurance, 401k, or other items. What's left is what we live on —you know, we need food, gas, clothes, insurance, utilities, transportation, healthcare, etc. For the most part, 42-45% is the high end of allowable DTI, because of all these other things not yet taken into consideration. Some loan programs, such as FHA loans will allow DTIs up to 55% or more. However, they also count the debt payments from your spouse, even if he/she is not on the loan. And, if any aspect of your loan causes your file to require a manual underwrite vs an automated approval, your max DTI can be as low as 50%.

VA loan programs may allow for higher debt ratio, but they also use formulas to deduct your income tax obligation from the equation, along with the projected cost of utilities, based on the home's square footage.

So, each loan program regards DTI differently, and the

kind of loan program that best suits you, has a lot to do with your DTI number. Make sure you are dealing with a lender that can offer you many different loan programs and is familiar with each of them.

Because government loans are stricter on the lender, many mortgage companies can't offer them. They will always try to offer borrowers conventional loans, but if their debt ratio is too high, they simply get denied. They are not typically going to say that you really could be approved on another type of loan, if only they offered it. You may walk out feeling that you just can't buy the home right now, when in reality, you can, but they aren't equipped to help you.

Some people may be surprised and ask, 'How can I have a high debt ratio, when I have no debt?' A lot of people feel this way because they don't realize what they have to count as debt.

For instance, let's say you have a home that your family member is living in, paying you rent monthly, but you are paying the mortgage. Unless you can show rental income on that property, you still have to count the mortgage, taxes, insurance, & HOA (Homeowners' Association Dues) in your monthly debt. If you are collecting rent on a property, talk to your CPA about including that in your tax return. It can help you avoid having to count that debt and can even give you write-offs. Most often, the rent is not income, but rather a break even or even a loss. Of course, a loss would have to be deducted from your income, so that has to be taken into consideration, as well.

Some lenders still don't know this, but in some cases if you have over 30% equity in your home, have a lease agreement, and have collected a deposit towards the rent, you may be able to use the rental amount to offset the existing mortgage on the home, even if it is not yet on the tax return. This would be allowed for a newly attained property or one that was previously your primary residence. This was done regularly in the past, then done away with, then brought back with modifications. That's why many don't realize it. Being able to offset a mortgage can greatly help your DTI issues.

What if your late spouse had the mortgage in their name only? Nothing showing on your credit report, but you are living in the home and paying the mortgage? Yes, you must count the home expense in your debt ratio until it is sold.

There are many other things that need to be counted in your debt ratio, which you may not think of. Child support that you are paying would be counted. If you are going for a VA loan, you may even have to count projected estimates for the utility bills in the new home, based on the square footage. Another thing that must be counted for VA loans is child care expenses. That can be a big one!

This is why it is so important to be thorough in your loan application. Work with a lender that knows the right questions to ask, and remember, things will come up in Underwriting, even if not disclosed up front, so it is best to be open and honest, and not have a disaster later. One of the keys to a smooth transaction is a complete loan application from the beginning.

Again, make sure you choose your lender carefully and that they have all the tools to help you!

Low on Funds?

Gifts, Down Payment Assistance, 401k Loans

Ready to buy a home, but down payment has you concerned?

Some people use different sources for their down payment funds. Here are some things you should know...

When applying for a mortgage loan, you will be asked how much you have on deposit for down payment and other related closing costs. If any of the funds in your account were recently deposited from a family gift or loan from your retirement account, be sure and disclose that right up front.

Where your money comes from is very important. For instance, it may be fine to have gift funds when buying a primary residence, but if you are buying an investment property, they may not be allowed. Depending on how much you put down on your primary residence, and what loan program you are in, you may be able to get 100% of your funds from gift, or you may have to show that a certain percentage was yours.

You don't want to get prequalified with your funds on deposit and then when your lender looks at your bank statement and sees that there is a deposit from gift funds, has to tell you that you have a problem and can't close on your loan.

The more info you can give up front, the better off you will be. If in doubt whether something is important or not, disclose it!

Down payment assistance programs are available through many different municipalities, and all come with their own requirements. Keep in mind, that with these programs, you will have to be approved by the lender for the loan, and by the assistance program for the down payment funds. Just because you are approved for one, doesn't mean you will be approved for the other. Some also require repayment of the funds, require you to live in the home for a certain number of years after closing, may require the home to be in a certain neighborhood, and may require your household income to be below a certain amount.

401k loans are also used to borrow funds for closing, when buying a home. These loans are not counted in your debt ratio, because you are technically paying yourself back. If you should leave your job prior to the 401k loan being paid in full, the loan may be due in full at that time.

Discuss where your down payment funds are coming from with your lender, to be sure you are making the best possible choice for your specific situation. For instance, if you know you will not be at your job long enough to pay back that loan, the 401k loan may not be the best option.

Gift funds are allowed on many loans, as long as the donor is a certain relationship to the borrower, and their documentation is in order, per loan guidelines. This was also discussed in previous sections of this book.

Case in point:
I had a client that had multiple deposits into his account from his parents. We had to get a gift letter from his parents, stating that this was not a loan, and that he did not have to repay the money. If we were doing a conventional loan, we would have been just fine, but since we were doing an FHA loan, we also needed to see his parent's bank statements, showing that the funds were seasoned in their account, prior to the gifts. In other words, that they had the money for a couple of months and didn't just deposit a large sum of unexplained assets in the accounts. Well, they were having no part of that. They absolutely refused to give us their bank statements, so the Underwriter had to back the total of all the gifts out of his current balance. This caused him to not have enough documentable funds to close. He actually had to wait 2 months to be able to provide 2 months of bank statements that did not have any undocumented deposits. He was very lucky that the seller of the home had already moved and didn't need to close in a hurry. Many would not be so lucky and the seller would just move on to another buyer. This is why getting a head start on your

mortgage loan is a good idea.

This will be discussed in greater detail later, but there are some loans that require very little money out of pocket. In fact, if you consider that it can take 2-3 months of rent (first month/last month/security deposit) to get into a new apartment or rental home, you may be able to buy a home for less out of pocket. And, you typically won't have a mortgage payment due in the first full month you live in the home.

Conventional loans start at 5% down; FHA loans start at 3.5% down; and VA and USDA loans, can be closed with no down payment. If you still don't have enough for down payment, some loans also allow for gift funds from certain family members, towards down payment. On a conventional loan, all of your down payment can be gifted and the only documentation needed is proof of transfer from their account to yours (or to the title company), along with a signed gift letter.

For FHA loans, all down payments may be gifted, as long as the donor doesn't mind providing a copy of their bank statement. This can be very invasive to some people, so make sure you ask right up front, or you will have an issue.

Once you have the down payment taken care of, there are still closing cost requirements, which can be several thousand dollars more. The good news is that even if your donor can't give you that much more, the seller is able to contribute to your closing costs. For instance, on most loans, the seller is allowed to contribute between 3 and 6% of the purchase price towards your closing costs. That's in addition to any costs that are the seller's responsibility already, per the contract. In the case of a VA or USDA loan, this could mean getting into the home with virtually no out of pocket. In the case of FHA or conventional, you may also get in with no out of pocket, if you utilize a combination of gift funds and seller contributions.

Low on Monthly Cash Flow?

Maybe you have enough money in the bank, but your concern is the new monthly payment.

A home payment can be much more than you are used to paying in rent.

Some ways to control that 'payment shock' is to look at your options—that is, options with regard to price, insurance premiums, and interest rates, in particular.

You will shop for your own insurance, and there are options when it comes to premiums. By looking at different deductible amounts, and different coverage options, you can see premiums for the same home that vary by $100-200/month. Also, when it comes to mortgage rates, you have the options to 'buy down' the rate by paying discount points up front. Lowering your rate by .5% on a sizable loan amount, can save you another significant amount monthly. Of course, if you cut these items as much as possible, and you are still not comfortable with the payment, the other areas to consider are more down payment; a lower purchase price; a neighborhood with lower tax rates; or a neighborhood with lower HOA dues. Remember, condos may be less expensive than single family homes, but can carry HOA dues that are hundreds of dollars per month vs. hundreds of dollars per year! What you don't want to do is get in over your head. Your lender may say you can afford the home, but all they can see are the debts on your credit report. They don't know how many sporting or other extracurricular activities your kids are into; how much you enjoy eating out; how many weekends a month you like to travel, etc. If you are not willing to drastically change your life for your house payment, you should make sure that the increase will not either impede your ability to enjoy your lifestyle, or cause you to get buried in credit card debt in order to keep it.

Never Paid for Living Expenses Before?

This is a very interesting group of people. Those who have been living at home and have not paid rent before. Going from this situation, straight in to buying a home, has its own set of challenges.

For instance, you may not have any idea what it takes to maintain a residence, or how much it can cost.
Also, if you have been living rent-free for years, I would hope that means you have a significant amount of money in your bank account. If not, you have to ask yourself the following questions…

"If I have been spending all my money each month, and not saving any of it, what am I going to do without, in order to pay my mortgage?"

"If I have to stop eating out, going out with friends, shopping, etc., just to be able to pay for a home, am I going to be happy?"

"Will I have extra money for the unexpected things that come up with home ownership, such as air conditioning, plumbing, roofing, or other repairs?"

If the answer is no to any of the above, you should have a really serious conversation with your significant other or a really deep meditation on the subject, if you are doing it alone. Now, I'm not suggesting that you should never fly from the nest, but I don't want to see you fail either. Make sure you have a safety net to catch you. The last thing you want to do is fly from the nest and then fall back into it.

Section 3:

Choosing the Right Loan and Lender

VA, FHA, USDA, Conventional, Jumbo, Fixed, Adjustable, 30 year, 20 year, 15 year, 10 year... How do you know which is best for you?

The short answer is to hire a professional mortgage lender and let them work with you to determine the best plan of action. DO NOT SHOP FOR A RATE, SHOP FOR A LOAN OFFICER—one that responds to you, has patience and knowledge, and has a great system in place to handle your loan. Then, let him/her shop for your rate/program.

A retail bank does their own Underwriting, but only

has a limited number of loans to offer you. If you don't fit the criteria for their programs, you will leave with a denial, and the impression that you cannot buy a home. In reality, you just can't buy a home WITH THEM.

A broker has many different loan programs available and will send your file to the program that is best suited for you. They will rely on the investor to underwrite the loan, and all investors are a bit different. This can cause the loan officer to submit something damaging, or not submit something helpful.

A correspondent lender offers programs from many different banks and mortgage companies and has in-house processing AND underwriting. So regardless of loan program, your loan officer will be familiar with the requirements and preferences of your Underwriter. They allow for the smoothest and quickest transactions. Best of both worlds!

There is a lot for you and your lender to consider and you should be in on the decision-making process, as I mentioned in the previous section. There are a few easy questions to answer that will help your loan officer guide you to the right loan program.

1. Are you a US Veteran? Disabled US Veteran?
2. Do you have a lot of money on deposit in your bank account(s)?
3. Do you have a good amount of monthly cash flow

from your income?
4. How long do you plan to own this home?

Believe it or not, these simple questions, will help to eliminate the worst and narrow down the best options for your loan program. It's not as scary as you think, when you take it step by step. Do FHA, VA and USDA loans scare you? Government red tape? Maybe, but with rates much lower than conventional, it may be worth it; especially, if you are working with a lending professional who is well versed in FHA and VA loans. The tape may not be as red as you think!

Loan Types

USDA (United States Department Of Agriculture)

These government loans are normally available for properties in more rural, outlying areas. They also have certain income restrictions for the borrowers. These requirements will vary, depending on county. It is always a good idea to ask if the property you are purchasing is eligible for this type of financing and if your income is too high to qualify. If the property is eligible, and you meet the qualifications, you are in for a real treat!

Check for address and borrower eligibility here: https://eligibility.sc.egov.usda.gov/eligibility/welcomeAction.do

THE ~~ROADS~~ ROAD to HOME OWNERSHIP & FINANCIAL FREEDOM

These loans:

Require NO down payment!
Carry no monthly mortgage insurance!
Still offer very competitive interest rates!

If you are narrowing down your home choices and one of the last homes in the running is USDA eligible and one is not, it could be a deciding factor.

For instance, a $200k home purchase comparison can look like this.

95% **conventional loan**	100% **USDA loan**
$190k loan amount	$200k loan amount
$10k for down payment	$0 for down payment
*$1020/month for Principal & Interest	*$1073/month for P&I
**$93 for mortgage insurance	$0 MI

So, you could potentially save $10k up front, and not have to carry MI, for 5 or 7 years.

 *based on 5% interest rate and 5.3% APR;

**based on .59% annual MI factor

VA/VALB (Veterans Administration / Veterans Administration Land Board)

THE ~~ROADS~~ ROAD to HOME OWNERSHIP & FINANCIAL FREEDOM

If you are a US Veteran, first of all – Thank you!

Secondly, you owe it to yourself to consider a VA/TX Veterans Land Board loan. This loan is only available to our Veterans. Like the USDA loan, there is no down payment, or monthly MI, but there are no property or income caps that the USDA loans carry.

You will need to provide your DD-214 and certificate of eligibility to verify your exact benefits. In many cases, disabled veterans won't even be required to pay the up-front funding fee that is normally rolled into your loan amount, and that can save you several thousands of dollars.

When using the VALB loans, your property and credit requirements will be much more lenient, your closing costs will be partially covered by the seller, and you will receive a discount to your rate, with a disability over 30%. National Guardsman and reservists on this program will be able to waive their interest while on active duty.

You earned your benefits, make sure you use them.
However, there are some cases when even a veteran can be better served with an alternative to the VA loan. Discuss your preferred down payment preferences with your lender and have them research all your loan options for you.

I once had a veteran client who was doing well for himself in his post-service career, and he was interested in buying a very expensive home. He needed to put 20% down, in order to keep his monthly payment in the approvable range. That removed the benefit of no down payment and MI on the VA loan. So, we decided to go conventional, to not go through the extra paperwork involved with the VA loan process, AND since he was not disabled, to avoid the up-front funding fee, which would have been over $10k on that particular loan amount. It's quite possible that if he were talking to another loan officer, he might have not been given the option, because many lenders automatically think VA, when they hear their client is a veteran. In many cases, that's the right way, but not always.

FHA   (Federal Housing Administration)

FHA is another government-backed loan program.

People normally lean towards this loan:

- When they prefer to spend less out of pocket for down payment and closing costs. There is only a minimum requirement of 3.5% for down payment. The seller is allowed to pay all closing costs and prepaid items over and above down payment, up to 6% of the sales price. Normally, costs are in the 3% range, so they can easily pay all other costs, as long as it is outlined in the sales contract. Please keep in mind that if the seller agrees to pay your closing costs, and you increase your purchase price, the appraised value must be equal to, or more than, your total purchase price. If it comes in low, the first thing to go when renegotiating will likely be the seller's contributions to your closing costs.

- If they have had credit issues in the past. This loan is much more lenient when it comes to credit score. The minimum credit score required can change, and the individual investor has a say in what they require, but it is usually much lower than a conventional credit score requirement and doesn't penalize lower scores with higher rates.

- If they don't have a lot of disposable income left at the end of each month. This loan program also allows a borrower's debt-to-income ratio to be much higher than a conventional loan program. One thing to remember is that government loans require that the debt of both spouses be counted, even if they are not both on the loan. So, the higher debt ratio allows for that.

So, why doesn't everyone go for this loan, and make their underwriting process so much easier?

The simple reason is that, the mortgage insurance that is required on these loans does not go away once a certain level of equity is accumulated. On a minimum 3.5% down payment transaction, the monthly MI will be charged for the lifetime of the loan. If you happen to put 10% down, the MI may drop off after 11 years. But, in many cases, the MI and lower interest together is still better than the higher conventional rates. This changes from time to time, so it's a good idea to compare the two, if you qualify for both.

If you have challenges with assets, income, or credit score, and want to buy a home, the FHA program may be the answer for you. If you do not have these challenges to the degree that conventional lending is out of reach, you may be better served going in that direction.

However, if the rate and MI is less on the FHA loan, and you are only going to live in your home for 5-7 years, you may still decide this is the best option for you. Even on conventional loans, the MI is usually collected for at least that long. Something to consider is that even though FHA allows up to 57% backend ratio (all debt vs income), many times you are capped at a 47% frontend ratio (home only vs income). So, make sure the home alone, even with no other debt, is not too much for your income. This is another place where the FHA is much more lenient than conventional, where you may be capped at 40% frontend ratio.

If you would like to know how much home you qualify for, make sure to ask a lender who is well versed in all guidelines (Conventional, Jumbo, FHA, VA, USDA). That way, you will be sure they offer you the best you qualify for, and not just the best they have to offer. This is one of those topics to discuss with your professional loan officer.

You may be starting to see why shopping for a loan officer is much more valuable to you than shopping for rates. Any good loan officer will get you the best rate you qualify for, but you have to first find the right loan program, level of customer service, and knowledge to really come out on top!

Conventional & Jumbo

Conventional loans are the 'vanilla' loans of the mortgage world. They are straightforward, based on traditional qualifications such as credit and income, and they reward higher scoring buyers with better rates. These loans generally require 5, 10 or 20% down payment. Any loan with less than 20% down payment, will require Mortgage Insurance (MI). This insurance is for the protection of the lender only. It allows the lender to offset some risk that is associated with less than 20% down payment. If the buyer is in default, the MI insurance company will pay the lender part of the amount due to them. That makes it easier for the mortgage company to sell the home quickly and still make enough to cover the rest. Before mortgage insurance was introduced to the lending world, mortgage loans always required 20% down. This is because lenders felt that a borrower would do everything possible to avoid foreclosure, if they have that much of their hard-earned money invested in the home.

Now, 80% Conventional loans can be combined with a 2nd lien to avoid MI and still borrow more than 80%. Of course, the rates are higher to make the loan interesting to the lender, in the absence of mortgage insurance. In addition, rates on the 2nd liens are even higher because the investor is not protected as much as the 1st lien holder, in the case of a default.

Jumbo loans are considered non-conforming conventional loans. These loans are for loan amounts higher than what are considered 'conforming loan limits' for the area. These limits are set by county. These Jumbo loans can require more down payment (typically 20% minimum), higher scores, and lower debt-to-income ratios than their conforming conventional counterparts.

Case in Point:
I had a client purchasing a home that would have had him fall into the Jumbo arena with the standard 20%

down. He had been denied elsewhere because his credit score and debt ratio were not in the approvable range for the Jumbo investors. When I reviewed his file, I noticed that if he just put down an extra $20,000, he would be below the conforming limit and his score and debt ratio were fine for a conforming loan. He had plenty of money on deposit, and although he didn't necessarily want to put $20k more into the deal, it was the difference between being able to buy the home, and not. But, he was never given the option, just a denial!

Programs for Teachers, Firefighters, Police, or any other group.

No one likes to be grouped together, as though they are not an individual, just because they belong to a group. There are loan programs that market to certain groups, such as first responders, nurses, teachers, etc...

It sounds like, "Oh, I belong to that group, so that must be something awesome for us, which no one else can get."

In reality, the program may have features that others do not, but it doesn't mean that you need those features, and you are likely paying more for the loan because of them.

For instance, not all nurses are the same. Some are new,

some are seasoned. Some are single, some have families. Some have good credit, some have not-so-good credit. Some have money saved for down payment, some have none. There cannot possibly be one loan that is best suited for all nurses. It's simply a marketing strategy to get that industry's business. So, if you see a program that offers help with down payment, that's great if you need help with down payment. If you see a loan that caters to lower scores or higher debt ratio, that's great if you need that. But, if you don't, you will get better terms with a different loan program. Don't fall for the marketing. Find a loan officer that you trust, whom you like working with, who has the patience to answer your questions, who has access to many different loan programs, and then let them go to work to find you the best loan FOR YOU. That is their job!

How Many Things Can Go Wrong? Let Me Count the Ways...

How many people are involved in your mortgage transaction?

Loan Originator
Loan Originator's Assistant
Lock desk
Disclosure Specialist
Set up Assistant
Processor
Underwriter
Underwriter's assistant
CD specialist
Closer

Not to mention, the 3rd party providers and others outside of the mortgage company

Realtors
Transactions coordinators
Appraiser
Inspector
Surveyor
Insurance agent
Title Co
Attorneys
HOA management companies

THE ~~ROADS~~ ROAD to HOME OWNERSHIP & FINANCIAL FREEDOM

Every employer you've worked for in the last 2 years (hope you left on good terms)
The SS administration and the IRS

It's amazing that anyone ever closes on time. If just one person in the mix is not doing a good job, it can throw off everything!

In an effort to simplify this process, and have fewer cooks to 'spoil the soup,' I have been able to cut the first-nine positions into 4! Each team member carries a bigger piece of the pie, because they are working on fewer files, overall. They take ownership in the process and are as intent on closing your loan as you are. Plus, the 3rd party providers I work with are among the best in the business. So, if you want me to help you find the right overall team, we can do that too.

Unfortunately, I still can't do anything about your past employers or the IRS! But, I'm still thinking! :)

Underwriters and Letters of Explanation

Many people wanting to buy a home, think that a gap in employment history is a kiss of death for their loan approval. But, that may not be the case. Many times, a good explanation is all that is needed. Sometimes, it's even a good thing. For instance, if you lose a job and it's taking an especially long time to find another, you may consider taking some classes to further your education, either in your field or a new one. If this results in a job, even if in a new field, you may still be fine to get a loan approval. Provide a good letter of explanation, stating that instead of taking an inferior job, you decided by advancing yourself you would be in a position to get a better one, and it worked.

Underwriters are not trying to deny your loan, but they have to make sure the documentation fits the requirements set out by the investor, and that the loan is sellable on the secondary market. It's all in the way it is presented.

An experienced loan officer doesn't just collect your documentation and throw it into underwriting. They should be presenting that file in a way that tells the borrower's story in the best possible light.

If you have a specific situation that needs to be looked at, let me know. I'd be happy to look at it for you and we can come up with the best plan of action.

Hopefully, you see why having a reliable, trustworthy team on your side is imperative on your journey towards home ownership and becoming financially free. Having the right team, at the right time, can save you thousands!

Section 4:

Buying or Building

First Home You Will Ever Buy?

A lot of what was said in the last section, can be said here as well.

If you have the money to put 20% down on a home, but you are drowning in other debt, you may consider a lower down payment, in order to pay off other things. If you have student loans, car payments, or credit card payments that add up to $600/month, and they can be paid off with $20,000 of that $40,000 you have set aside for down payment, you may consider using it that way. Your mortgage payment will not increase by that much, due to less down payment, so using the money that way will free up much more monthly cash flow and stop the interest from building on the other loans.

$20,000 more on your mortgage may only be $100/month more in payment, but getting rid of that $20,000 in other debt can free up as much as $600/month!

You would be $500/month ahead of the game. If you then applied it to your new mortgage, you would pay it off in a fraction of the time and save thousands in interest there too. The nice thing is as your family grows, or life becomes more expensive, you may not be able to pay that extra $500/month to the mortgage, and you are not obligated to do so. It's flexibility that you do not have with all the other bills hanging over your head.

So, instead of getting back into debt just to keep up with life, you just tap into your extra monthly cash flow.
The key here is to not dedicate that extra money to new debt, car payments, or loans, which MUST be paid each month. If you do that, there is no EXTRA any more. Keep your paycheck as liquid as possible, and then when you really need something, you don't have to borrow.

How cool would it be to buy that next car in cash?

Case in point:
I had a young couple, buying their first home, and they were so proud that they had 20% for the down payment. However, they have tens of thousands of dollars in student loan debt. After showing them the difference in mortgage payments, they decided to put only 5% down on the home, and use the rest to pay off debt. This saved them much, much more than it cost between the higher mortgage amount and mortgage insurance. It freed up a lot of money that they could put towards paying off the few debts that lingered and building up their savings for the future.

If this section isn't for you, refer back to the sections about being low on funds or monthly cash flow.

Building a Home is Not for Everyone

If you decide that you are up to the challenge of building a home vs. buying a pre-existing one, make sure to consider these important aspects of the deal.

- If you are "having a new home built" to your order, but the builder will construct on his dime, and then you will close once 100% complete, it's not much different than buying a pre-existing home; except it will take longer and you will likely be strong-armed into using their affiliated mortgage and title companies. Don't take the promised savings at face value. Many times, the fees they waive for you to use their companies, are not as much as the extra fees they tack on, or as much as the higher interest rates. You have every right to use the companies you choose and you should compare what the real savings are.

- If you are using a custom, independent builder, where you are responsible for the construction cost, make sure you consider the fact that the builder must be approved, as much as the borrowers. The lender has to be sure that they are handing that money over, during the construction phase, to a reputable company with the resources to get the job done right. Also, the draws are made AFTER the completion of each step, so there has to be some start-up money to begin the construction. If the borrower asks you to lay out the money to get started, as opposed to having a line of credit for that, you may want to think about how stable that builder is.

- Building a home will require 20% for down payment plus other costs. When you buy a pre-existing home, you can buy with as little as 3.5% down. And, last but not least, the longer the building project takes, the more interest you will be paying on the construction funds. Check out the builder's record for on-time completion. Remember, if they are building on their own dime, they are more motivated to complete on time, than if you are carrying the construction costs.

- If you already own the land you will build on free and clear, the value of the land will be used as your down payment for the construction loan. Usually, you will need at least 20% for down payment on the construction loan, so if your land is worth more than 20% of the total value of the construction and land combined, you may only have to bring your closing costs to closing.

Building a home can be very exciting, as you get to make it just as you like it. You pick out everything from the appliances, to the finishes, to where the electrical outlets will go. But it is not for the faint of heart. The more time you can spend overseeing the project, the better it will go, but it will take a lot out of your time and energy. It may not be the right choice for your first home. Just some things worth considering!

Happy house hunting!

Industry regulations change often.

For the most up to date answers to your questions, call a trusted mortgage professional today!

Section 5:

Positioning Yourself for Financial Freedom
&
Saving Thousands

Last Home You Will Ever Buy?

So, you have done this several times already, and now you are buying your final, rest-of-your-days home! Congratulations!

There is a lot to consider here, as well.

Many people sell a home, make a good amount of money from the sale, and put it all in to the next home. That is a good strategy, if you still have a lot of liquid assets to tap into, when needed. If not, you may be better off putting less into the new home and keeping some liquid assets available in case of emergency. No one knows what the future holds, and nothing speaks "stability and freedom" like cash in the bank!

The temptation to have a home free and clear is a great one. Don't get me wrong; paying off your home should be a goal, but it should be your last goal. What I mean by that is, if you are going to owe money anywhere, your home is the place to do it. Rates are among the lowest, the interest is usually tax deductible, and the payments are spread out so far, that they are the lowest possible monthly payments. So, the first goal should be to pay off all other debt. Then, have a savings or safety net that can get you through several months of bad times. Lastly, before you start pouring money into your home, make sure that your long-term plans/needs are taken care of.

For instance, do you have tuition money for a child going to school soon? Do you have enough to cover that wedding you will pay for, in the near future? Do you have the insurance you need in case the golden years have times of illness or health care requirements? If the answer is no to any of the above, you should get all that in order before paying off your home or putting all your money into a down payment for a new home.

If you pay off your home, and then have to borrow for other things, it is almost a given that the rates will be higher, the payments will be higher, and the interest you pay will not be tax deductible.

If all the above is in order, then by all means, pay that house off and live happily ever after! I've seen too many people put too much into a new home, or pay off a mortgage too quickly, without having these other things in order. Then they end up coming to me to borrow the equity from their home, in order to take care of these things. Well, this approach is fine, if you don't need the money tomorrow and don't mind paying to get it. And, if you still have the income to qualify for the loan. Please plan ahead!

Already Have Paid Off a Home?

If you already have a home that is free and clear, that is awesome! Especially if you are not still drowning in other debt, or have future expenses keeping you up at night. Financial freedom is a wonderful thing, but it should not be confused with paying off a home. You can have a mortgage-free home and still not be financially free. To be truly free, you have to have several things working for you…

1. You have no consumer debt — burning your mortgage note, but still paying for credit cards, loans, or other debts each month doesn't feel like freedom, does it?

2. You have an emergency fund that you can literally live on for months, if necessary.

3. Your long-term needs fully funded.

4. Then, a mortgage-free home.

Once you have all this lined up, you can feel truly free. Most people work on paying off the home first, when that should be closer to the bottom of the list. In fact, the equity in your home, can fast forward you on your way to financial freedom. Most of my clients that use the equity in their home are on track to true financial freedom in 5-10 years of borrowing that equity. And, that includes paying off the new 30-year mortgage! Read more about this in the "The Real Value to Your Home Equity" subsection.

Selling a Home? Don't Get Too Excited!

When selling a home, you may find yourself with a large amount of cash on hand after closing. You may be tempted to do many things with that money...

Put a large down payment on your next home
Pay off all your other debts
Take a trip
Invest in the stock market

But, stop and think first. Remember, it may be one of the few times you will have that lump sum in hand. Think about your long-term needs. All the above are great ideas, but remember, once you 'write that check,' it's gone. Even if you put it in to the next home, you will have to go through an approval process, if you ever want to get your money back out. That is an expense you can avoid, with proper planning. Investments can be very rewarding, but also they come with a certain level of risk. Paying off debt is a great idea, as long as you make good use of the savings each month, and don't get back into debt. Otherwise, you will feel like your home equity went up in smoke.

My point is, take a breath and don't rush into anything. The money will not burn a hole in your bank account, I promise. You can always spend it later, but once it's gone, it's gone. There is no harm in hanging on to it. Buy your next home with limited down payment and if you decide later that your home is the best place for that money, you can make a principal reduction payment.

Things to consider when deciding what to do with your funds...
- Do I have a child going to college in the next several years? Will I need to help with their college expenses?

- Will my income be reducing due to retirement? Would a healthy savings account allow me to feel more confident in my retirement years?

- Do I have an aging parent with no long-term care insurance? Will the responsibility fall on me if they need assistance in their old age?

I make a living from originating loans, and I will be happy to offer you a home equity loan anytime you need one. However, my future income is not dependent on giving you bad advice. On the contrary, my clients know they can trust me to advise them, based on their best interests, not mine. So, if you want to test your scenario by leveraging my expertise, I would be happy to listen and make sure you consider all your options, before you spend your money. I also have a wonderful network of professionals who can advise you further on investing, college and/or retirement planning, insurance, estate planning, income tax, and anything else you may need. I only refer to people I would trust with my most valued clients or family!

Can't See the Forest for the Trees?

Would you pay a fee (even if it seemed expensive), if it meant you could totally change your life for the better?

Of course, you would!

If you would have said no, I would have referenced that old saying, "You can't see the forest for the trees." In other words, you are focusing on small details, which are stopping you from seeing the big picture.

Some people do this, when they say that they don't

want to refinance their home loan, due to having to pay closing costs again.

I understand not wanting to pay fees. I don't like them either. But, I have refinanced my own home a couple of times (and yes, I do pay the fees, too). That's because of the forest!

First off, you must realize that you are not paying again for the same loan. Your new loan is completely new. All the details that went into securing your last loan must be done again to secure your new one. And everyone involved, from the appraiser to the title company, wants to get paid. No one I know works for free.

What you must realize is that if you are mortgaging your home again, there must be a significant benefit. You may be setting yourself up to save a lot of money monthly, or over the life of the loan, or both. You may be tapping into funds you need for college, medical expenses, retirement, or investments. You may be going from having 25 more years left on your home, to becoming totally debt-free in 6-10 years. I have helped people with each of these scenarios, and although it's never fun to pay several thousand dollars in fees, you must look at the big picture. Plus, the fees associated with the new loan are not paid out of pocket. Most often, they are rolled into the new loan.

So, now when I ask, "would you spend $6, 7, or even 10k to save $100k?" you should say ABSOLUTELY! And I will say, "There's someone who can see the forest!"

The Real Value to Your Home Equity

Most of us can't wait to pay off our home, but don't think twice about owing our whole paycheck to creditors before we even get it. If you can retrain that way of thinking, you can literally change your life. For quite some time, I have been teaching people how to become debt-free (including their home mortgage), by leveraging the funds they are paying to debt on a monthly basis.

Most of my clients, who have chosen to use this equity, are on a plan to become debt free in 8-10 years, versus the 20 or more years they currently have left on their homes, and the countless years of miscellaneous debt that is consuming their paychecks every month. All of this comes with only committing the same amount they are already spending each month, and many times less (no increase to total monthly debt payment amount).

Case in Point:
I had a client who wanted to refinance her mortgage to lower the payment. There was only about $35,000 left on the note, so the savings were far from earth shattering, considering she would be starting over for 30 years. When I questioned her on what she was really trying to accomplish, I found out that money was tight because of all their other debt and it seemed it would never go away. So, after crunching the numbers, I suggested that she borrow the equity in the home to pay off all the other debt. In all, it was about $70k worth of cars, credit cards, and loans. It freed up almost $1800/month and the new mortgage payment was even less than the old one, so that was even more savings each month.

Next, we figured out how much of that savings they could comfortably add to the new mortgage payment (being sure to keep enough cash to avoid the use of credit). They started applying that extra money to the principal balance, and do you know what happened?

They paid off the home in 6 short years! All the other debt was gone, and now the mortgage, too. They retired, sold the home, took the cash, and bought a lake home (without a mortgage)! Talk about living happily ever after!

So, think about it… do you just want your home to be paid off, or do you want to be debt-free and no longer a slave to creditors for the rest of your life? It is more realistic than you think! And, the best part is, the more debt you are already paying each month, the better this works. Because you are already used to paying that much more, so there are more resources to turn towards the home.

If you are thinking of putting a large down payment into your upcoming home purchase, but have other debt, please call me. With this technique, I can show you how to pay off your home and become free of other debt in a much shorter amount of time, and/or save a lot of money on a monthly basis.

Helping people become debt-free is truly my passion. We all need loans at certain times in our lives, but that doesn't mean we need to have them hanging over our heads forever.

When You Inherit a Home, the Gift May Be More Than "Just" a Free Home

When a relative gifts you a home, or you inherit one, that is free and clear, you may be thinking, "Great, no mortgage payments for life!" But, if you are eyeball deep in debt already, you may be thinking, "I need to sell it and get the money."

But, before you do anything rash, consider another option. Texas' home equity refinance loans (and many other states) allow you to tap into the equity in the home, without having to sell it. So, if that home has been in your family forever, and it would kill you to sell it, you don't have to. You can still hit the reset button on your finances.

Consider this...

A home that was bought 50 years ago for $100k in a nice neighborhood and has been paid off for decades, may today be worth $500k. What if you have $200k in student loans and other debt, and you are paying almost $3000/month, with nothing to show for it? You are still renting an apartment with a roommate because that's all you can afford without going bankrupt.

Here's what you do...

Take out a $300 - $400k loan against the home (you can do this in as little as 6 months of being on title); pay off ALL your debt; your mortgage will be less than what you were already used to paying those other creditors;

you'll have $100 - $200k left over to fix the place up (you may love the childhood memories, but not Grandma's wallpaper) and start a nice savings; and you'll have a great home. Best of all, no more roommates and no more living paycheck to paycheck.

Furthermore, if you take what you used to pay in rent and add it to the mortgage payment, you will pay that family home off in half the time (some of my clients who use this strategy are completely debt-free in 6-10 years.

So, before you make any fast decision, in this or any other life event, make sure you talk to a professional who can help you figure out the best game plan for your specific scenario. I have been doing this for my clients for years and the success stories are truly inspiring! Many loan officers are just what I call order-takers. A client calls and states their interest in a conventional loan, a rate/term refinance, or 20% down for a home, the Loan Officer says, "yes, ma'am," when, in reality, the client would be better served with an FHA loan, a cash out refinance, or by putting just 5% down. I don't want to be an order taker. I want to be a trusted advisor. The ultimate decision is the client's to make, but I wouldn't be doing my job, if I didn't make sure they understood ALL their options!

Call me... Maybe your story will be in my next book!

Section 6

Buyer Beware

Taxes, Insurance, & Homeowners' Associations – I thought I had a Fixed Rate Loan!

Many people think that because they have a fixed rate loan, their payment will never change. That's partially true. The principal and interest portion of the loan payment will not change. But lenders don't have any control over changes to your taxes or insurance amounts. If your payment on a fixed rate loan has changed, that's probably the reason why.

The good news is, your escrow account has a small "cushion" built in to help with these increases. And, even if that cushion is not enough, and you end up with a shortage in your account, your bills will still be paid. Your lender will pay the bills, and as well let you know of the shortage amount and the new payment amount that will be implemented in order to 1) pay back the shortage and 2) have enough in the account for next year's bills. It's like an interest-free loan for your tax/insurance bills to be paid in full and on time. For those who don't escrow for taxes or insurance, your payment will not change (P&I), but you will be responsible for coming up with the increased amounts on your own, when due.

If you are very responsible and it is customary for you to have thousands in the bank at year end that are not needed for other expenses, you may choose to waive escrows when applying for your mortgage loan (some loan terms don't allow for waiver). But if this is a financially stressful time of the year with the holidays, HOA dues, and income tax season right around the corner, setting up an escrow account may be a way to remove one more piece of the 'stress puzzle'.

Property taxes are a large part of your mortgage payment or obligation, even if not included in your payment. Make sure you are aware of what this expense will be before choosing your home. Make sure you file for your homestead exemption, if your state offers one, to get a discount on your primary residence tax bill. Take advantage of any other exemptions such as Veteran, disability, or over-65 that you may qualify for. It is up to you to know when your exemption application is due and if you miss it, you have to wait another year to apply. That's why I make it a habit to call all my clients to remind them when they need to take care of these important things. Once a buyer moves into the home, they go on with life, and these types of deadlines are not first and foremost on their mind, especially if it's the better part of a year before they can do it.

Insurance premiums are the next most expensive item, and can vary greatly from one insurance agency to another, as well as between all the different types of policies and coverages available. Work with an agent that can show you different options and explain what is, and more importantly, what IS NOT covered. The time you are making a claim is not the time to find out you selected a policy that doesn't cover your loss. Shop for your insurance, as soon as you select your home. If a home in that price range normally carries an insurance premium of $100/month, but your particular home has some issue that causes it to carry a premium of $250/month, the difference to your debt ratio can cause you to lose your approval. You don't want to wait until a week before closing to find out. Also, if you are in a flood zone, you will be obligated to get flood insurance, which can be a significant added expense. And, why take the chance that Mother Nature may delay you? Did you know that in the gulf coast states, if there is a named storm in the gulf, insurance companies stop writing policies until after it dissipates or downgrades. No insurance, no closing! Get your insurance lined up early!

Another type of insurance is mortgage insurance (MI) that you may be paying to cover your lender in case you default on your loan. This will be found included in your escrow payments. In some cases, this insurance may be dropped once you have a certain amount of equity in your home. Keep an eye on property values and your loan amount. When there is a 20% difference between the two, you can start working with your lender to have this MI removed. Of course, you must have a perfect payment history with them and an appraisal may be required to prove value. If your neighborhood values increase faster than predicted, you can be paying MI for years longer than you have to. That can be thousands of dollars, and it will not be refunded after the fact.

Homeowners' Association Dues (HOA) are usually paid yearly, and separately from your mortgage payment, but the monthly portion is counted in your debt-to-income ratio. Some properties don't have any HOA, some have a very small annual fee, and some can be hundreds per month, as in the case of condos. That's why we mentioned before how important it is to keep your lender involved in any possible property type changes.

All these items play a huge part in your household expense. Address them early on in the mortgage process, and do annual check-ups on your insurance. The most cost-effective policy this year, may not be the best next year. If you need a referral to an insurance agent who works like me (has the ability to shop many different companies to find you the best), let me know. If your agent can only represent one insurance company, they are working for that company, and not for you. They are not going to tell you that you can do better elsewhere. But, if your agent has dozens of companies to offer you, they have no motivation to not get you the best you qualify for and deserve.

Keep an eye on your yearly property tax statement. If you feel your property has been given more value than is realistic, you can request a review to have the tax value lowered. A real estate professional in your area can give you the ammunition you need to fight that value. Taxes, if not monitored, can get out of hand and you will only realize it when it affects your mortgage. Don't let over-zealous tax appraisers cause you to lose control of your home!

Beware of Agreements to be Signed Outside of Closing

I'm including this section, because I recently heard about a practice that apparently is common in the new home arena. Let's say you buy a model home from a builder. You are asked to lease it back to the builder until they are done building in the neighborhood, because they need to continue using it as their office. You are asked to sign a lease agreement for 6-18 months! That would be fine if you bought the home as an investment (rental) property, but if you bought it as a primary residence, you would be committing mortgage fraud (unknowingly of course).

I'm writing this because most people would have no idea that this is a problem. When you buy a home as a primary residence, one of the disclosures you sign at closing states that you MUST occupy the home within 60 days of closing. If the lender finds out that you didn't move in within that time frame, they can call the note due and payable. Unless you have the money on deposit to pay the loan off within a moment's notice, this can be a problem. This can occur by random audit, or if someone is smart enough to note that they are still sending your mortgage statements to your previous address after closing. There are many ways they can find this out. They may not, but they certainly can. Do you really want to worry about this?

The reason lenders care so much about your intention for the property is that investment properties must be funded with different loan programs which require more down payment and different rates. Investment properties are riskier than primary residences. People will do anything possible to avoid foreclosure of the roof over their heads, but investment properties are easier to let go, when times get hard. Unless, of course, you have more money invested in it, hence the different loan requirements.

So, if you are asked to sign a lease agreement that wasn't included in the docs that are going to the lender,

BEWARE! Any amendments, addendums, or other agreements must be made available to the underwriter in advance of loan approval, and provided to the investor after closing.

In the end, if this is discovered, the buyer would be the responsible party, not the builder. The builder is not required to know mortgage rules, or advise the buyer of them. The buyer, however, is required to be truthful on the loan application.

In Closing, it would be impossible to teach you all I know about the mortgage loan process in a book, regardless of the size. This short, easy read, is intended to give you a basic overview, allow you to realize that there is a lot to consider with mortgage finance, inspire you to ask questions about your specific scenario, and most importantly, help you choose an experienced lender with a teaching spirit, to guide you through the process and help you uncover the answers.

If you are in the great state of Texas, and would like my assistance with any mortgage related questions, I would be honored to help you!

Thank you for reading!

Now, hear what others have to say…

"As you may remember (builder) was really wanting us to finance with them and made it difficult to see clearly what we truly needed to do. I've noticed, while going through the paperwork, how much more contact we had with you and how you were there for us at a moment's notice to help us. So, I wanted to take a few minutes to say THANK YOU again for being our advocate and helping us to purchase our home! It means the world to us and we are so grateful for all your time and efforts!" -Cyndi & Steve Y.

"My loan application was for a jumbo loan, so I naturally assumed big, high risk for the lender, and it would take long to close, due to the additional due diligence. This would be the situation in most cases. However, because of JoAnn's in-depth knowledge on the whole process, the time it took to process the loan went a lot quicker than I expected. In addition to that, the communication and contact with JoAnn was superb. I knew how my loan was progressing every step of the way. My realtor was also pleasantly surprised, having worked with many loan officers, she commented JoAnn delivered 1st class service." -Bola O.

I have never seen a better combination of professional expertise, knowledge, tenacity, attitude, patience, and personal service in my 31 years as a Real Estate Broker!"
-Page Willis, Re/Max Cinco Ranch.

"JoAnn helped me with the purchase of my first home. She was super patient and guided me through the whole process. I had too many questions and although it took me some time to find the right place it was so worth it! If I had to do it all over again, I'd be confident having JoAnn on my side. I'll recommend her to all my friends!!!" - Pilar D.

"I worked with JoAnn to refinance my mortgage. She is a true professional - very knowledgeable, efficient, competent, organized and timely. She helped me select a product that was right for my financial situation and overall made the whole process stress free and not overwhelming. Pleasure working with you, JoAnn! Thank you!"
-Aleksandra L.

"This is our second service JoAnn has completed for us. Always top notch, and we will be back for more, when needed. She is our go to person from now on; we are that happy with her! We recommend her to our employees, business associates, and vendors when possible. She's top notch at customer service, as well as her whole team." - Gerald W.

"I enjoy working with JoAnn. She is very professional and detail oriented. I have used her services personally with the purchase of my current home and in cooperation with her on many mutual clients. I highly recommend her."   -Suzanne Sansom, Independent Insurance agent

"I just wanted to pause and thank you and your team for all that you have done to assist Scott and I on our first home purchase. Your professionalism and caring efforts have certainly provided us with much needed comfort during this process --- rather than being stressed, we are at ease and our excitement grows with each passing day. We count ourselves very fortunate to have you in our corner and are sure to tell anyone who will listen. Gratefully, Kimberly - P.S. Rianne (our realtor) also mentioned how impressed she was with you and your firm and asked where we found you! :) " - Scott & Kimberly K.

"We want to share what a wonderful experience that refinancing our home meant to Ted and I. When we first met with you we learned of how refinancing works, costs, details and this made it so easy for us to move forward with the refinance. We had a few extra bills that we decided to consolidate and boy that just freed up our finances and we only had one monthly bill with a much lower interest rate and monthly payment. Should we ever need to use your services again, we will not hesitate and of course we will refer our friends.

Thank you for being so informative each step of the way and for changing the way we feel about the mortgage industry. " -Ted & Melodie L.

"Wasn't even sure I would qualify for my own home. I reached out to JoAnn to get some advice on what steps I should take in order to do so and in a few months I was moving in! Couldn't have asked for better communication and customer service. I honestly felt like we were in this together and as a team we got my 1st home (and a beautiful one at that!). I'm just thrilled and so thankful to JoAnn and her associates!" -Shy M.

"John and I have been thrilled at the work JoAnn did for us this past year. She has excellent customer service and will walk you through anything you do not understand. There is nothing scary or intimidating about the process when you are in JoAnn's care!" -Tanya D.

JoAnn is a Senior Loan Officer with 1st NWM Corporation, and she is a 2016, 2017 & 2018 - 5 Star Professional Award Winner

Since 2003, JoAnn has been helping fellow Texans make their dreams come true – Not only home-ownership dreams, but their dreams of financial freedom, as well. This book is a compilation of some of the most important things you can know when home ownership – past, present, or future - is in your lifetime resume, and it demonstrates how to use your mortgage loans to your benefit.

Mailing address:
403 W Grand Pkwy S, Suite F-196
Katy, TX 77494

Physical address:
2744 Briarhurst Dr, #16
Houston, TX 77057

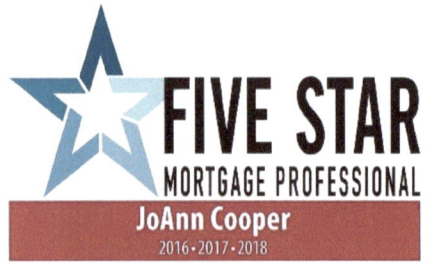

I know your family and friends would appreciate you sharing this book with them. There is something for everyone in these pages.

GET YOUR QUESTIONS ANSWERED BY A PROFESSIONAL:

All inquiries and presentation requests should be directed to: 281.948.3966 or

JoAnn@NationwideLendingPartners.com

Loan Officer NMLS# 300841 – Branch NMLS# 1437886

Notes:

Notes:

www.ingramcontent.com/pod-product-compliance
Lightning Source LLC
Chambersburg PA
CBHW040227220526
45473CB00001B/148